*This Annual belongs to*

*Princess*...................................................

(Write your name here)

**Editor:** Sally Gilbert
**Art Editor:** Alexandra Brown
**Photography:** Colin Bowling

© Disney Enterprises, Inc. All rights reserved. Published in Great Britain in 2004 by Egmont Books Limited, 239 Kensington High Street, London W8 6SA. Printed in Italy.
ISBN 1 4052 1385 X

Note to parents: adult supervision is recommended when sharp-pointed items such as scissors are in use.

# My

# Disney's

# Princess

## Annual 2005

Once upon a time, *Princess* ___Louise___
(write your name here)

was invited into a magical world where

she could become a princess with all her

favourite Disney Princesses.

# The Winter Summer Sun

One day, Snow White woke up feeling blue. She was missing the warmth of summer.

"Winter is lots of fun," she sighed, "but I do miss the golden feel of the summer sun."

The dwarfs decided to cheer her up. "Let's create the feel of summer by baking her a summer pudding!" suggested Happy. "The pudding will fill the cottage with the golden smell of summer."

The pudding was delicious and Snow White appreciated their efforts very much but it still didn't stop her wishing for summer.

"I wish we could sit outside on the lawn and eat our summer pudding amongst the flowers," she sighed. Wanting to please Snow White, the dwarfs went and had a look out of the window. Unfortunately, there was not a flower in sight and the ground was completely covered in snow.

"Let's get to work, boys," declared Grumpy.

The dwarfs marched out into the garden with their shovels, to scoop away all the snow. Then, they placed paper flowers all around the garden.

Snow White was delighted when she saw what they had done. "It's looks just like summer now," she giggled.

But as Snow White and the dwarfs ate their summer pudding in the cold garden, they couldn't stop shivering.

"It might look like summer but it

sure don't feel like it," chattered Doc.

Then, to make matters worse, a heavy snow shower soaked the paper flowers, making them soggy.

Back inside the cottage, Snow White tried to put on a brave face but the dwarfs could tell that she was disappointed.

"I guess I'll just have to wait until summertime to feel the golden glow of the sun again," she sighed.

The dwarfs looked at each other and grinned.

"We know where you can sit in the glow of sunshine all year around," laughed Happy.

The giggling dwarfs told Snow White to follow them. They led her out of the cottage, through the forest and to the diamond mine where

they worked.

"I can't sit in the sun underground?" puzzled Snow White.

"You can with our special golden sunshine," chuckled Bashful.

Once inside the mine, the heat from the dwarfs' lanterns made it feel cosy and warm.

Snow White gasped in wonder when she saw a golden throne in the main chamber of the mine.

The light from the lanterns and the jewels made the golden throne glow like the summer sun.

Snow White was thrilled, as she took her place on the glowing throne.

"The only thing missing are some summer songs," said Grumpy.

The dwarfs smiled, as they produced musical instruments and danced around Snow White on her wonderful summer throne.

**The End**

# Snow White

### Snow White and the Prince

The lovely Snow White has a charming childhood innocence about her that is reflected in her gentle ways and sweet manner. Her pure, loveable nature wins her the friendship and protection of the forest animals, the Seven Dwarfs and – of course – the handsome prince.

### The Seven Dwarfs

The Seven Dwarfs – Grumpy, Happy, Sneezy, Doc, Bashful, Sneezy and Dopey – live in a little cottage in the forest and work together in a diamond mine. They all care about Snow White and are ready to protect her at any cost.

### Forest Animals

When Snow White finds herself in the forest, she immediately wins the hearts of the forest animals, who help her find shelter in the Dwarfs' cottage. The forest animals soon become her good friends and she feels that she can confide in them. The animals love to listen to her singing, too.

# Flower Ring

*Make and wear this flower ring and become a forest princess.*

## You will need:

gold card & tinfoil

red sequins

glue

pencil

sticky tape

scissors

**1**

Draw a flower shape on gold card and carefully cut it out.

Glue balls of screwed-up tinfoil to the centre of the flower, then stick red sequins on the petals of the flower.

**2**

**3**

Cut a strip of gold card to fit around your finger and tape into a band shape. Tape the band to the back of the flower.

**Note to parents:** adult supervision is recommended when sharp-pointed items such as scissors are in use.

# Winter Teasers

**1** How many jewels are there below?

**2** There are three differences to the lower winter flower. Can you spot them?

**3** Which two lanterns below are exactly the same?

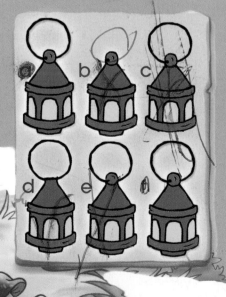

**4** How many tea cups would come next in the pattern?

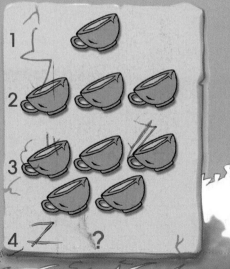

13

# January

| Monday | Tuesday | Wednesday | Thursday | Friday | Saturday | Sunday |
|--------|---------|-----------|----------|--------|----------|--------|
| | | | | | New Year's Day 1 | 2 |
| 3 | 4 | 5 | 6 | 7 | 8 | 9 |
| 10 | 11 | 12 | 13 | 14 | 15 | 16 |
| 17 | 18 | 19 | 20 | 21 | 22 | 23 |
| 24 | 25 | 26 | 27 | 28 | 29 | 30 |
| 31 | | | | | | |

Notes

# February

|  | 1 | 2 | 3 | 4 | 5 | 6 |
| 7 | 8 | 9 | 10 | 11 | 12 | 13 |
| Valentine's Day ♥ 14 | 15 | 16 | 17 | 18 | 19 | 20 |
| 21 | 22 | 23 | 24 | 25 | 26 | 27 |
| 28 | | | | | | |

Monday  Tuesday  Wednesday  Thursday  Friday  Saturday  Sunday

Notes

15

# The Spring Wish

One morning, Aurora woke up and instantly felt full of magical energy. She couldn't help singing and dancing around her room at the palace.

"What is this strange feeling inside of me?" Aurora thought to herself. "I can't wait to go outside and do things."

When Aurora met the fairies she asked them about the feelings she was experiencing.

"That's your spring wish coming to the surface!" giggled Fauna.

"My spring wish?" puzzled Aurora.

"Today is the first day of spring," explained Merryweather. "On this day, nature grants the most heart-felt wish to every living thing."

Just then, a group of small birds appeared and happily flew around Aurora. They whistled and tweeted a delightful tune into her ear.

"The birds wished for a new song," said Fauna, "and it came true."

16

"Let's go into the garden," suggested Flora, "and see if any other spring wishes have been granted."

Aurora was amazed, as she watched beautiful rosebuds appear on the bushes.

"The rose bush has wished for spectacular new blooms," chuckled Merryweather.

Aurora then noticed some cocoons on a nearby leaf. They began to shake and split open.

"The caterpillars are about to get their spring wish," cheered Flora.

Suddenly, a dozen dazzling butterflies emerged and fluttered all around the garden.

"How wonderful," laughed Aurora. "The caterpillars must have wished for

spectacular wings."

Aurora realised that the fairies were watching her and giggling.

"We were wondering what your spring wish will be?" they tittered.

"My spring wish?" said Aurora. "I have no idea."

"It must be a wish that comes from deep within your heart and will make you feel beautiful," explained Merryweather.

At first, Aurora wasn't sure what to wish for but then she listened to her heart and slowly began to smile.

"I want to wish for something that I have already," she announced, "because it always makes me feel beautiful."

The fairies were puzzled, as Aurora closed her eyes and wished.

Just then, Prince Phillip magically appeared in front of them.

Aurora sighed with delight, as the Prince stepped forward.

"You look beautiful, Aurora," said Prince Phillip and gave her a tender kiss.

The fairies giggled and blushed, as they left the happy couple alone.

"How lovely, Aurora's spring wish was for her prince," chuckled Flora.

"Judging by the look in Prince Phillip's eyes," laughed Fauna, "Aurora was his spring wish, too!"

## The End

# Aurora

## Aurora and Prince Phillip

Aurora is the daughter of King Stefan and the Queen. She is a graceful creature with a lovely voice and natural grace. But when a chance meeting with Prince Phillip in the woodland occurs, her yearning for romance causes her to throw caution to the wind.

## The Fairy Godmothers

Aurora's three Fairy Godmothers, Merryweather, Flora and Fauna, love the princess like a daughter. When Aurora was born, Flora gave her the gift of beauty and Fauna the gift of song, while Merryweather put limitations on Maleficent's curse.

## Woodland Creatures

The animals near the fairies' cottage in the forest are Aurora's friends. Aurora tells them all about her hopes and dreams.

## Maleficent

Maleficent lived in a castle on the Forbidden Mountain. She placed an evil curse on Aurora when she was born. Prince Phillip defeats Maleficent and breaks the curse.

# Spring Tiara

*Make and wear this tiara and you'll look as sweet as a spring rose.*

**1**

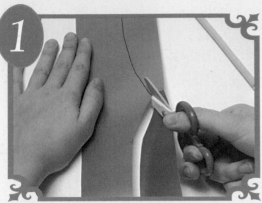

Draw a tiara shape on gold card and carefully cut it out.

## You will need:

gold card

pink & green felt

jewels  sticky tape

pencil  scissors  sequins  glue

**Note to parents:** adult supervision is recommended when sharp-pointed items such as scissors are in use.

**2**

Decorate the tiara by making and gluing on felt flowers, sequins and jewels.

**3**

Bend the tiara into shape, making sure it fits around your head, then tape in place.

Use the little picture inside the spring flower to
help you colour this page.

# March

|  | 1 | 2 | 3 | 4 | 5 | 6 |
|---|---|---|---|---|---|---|
| 7 | 8 | 9 | 10 | 11 | 12 | 13 |
| 14 | 15 | 16 | 17 | 18 **Good Friday** | 19 | 20 **Easter Sunday** |
| 21 | 22 | 23 | 24 | 25 | 26 | 27 |
| 28 | 29 | 30 | 31 | | | |

| Monday | Tuesday | Wednesday | Thursday | Friday | Saturday | Sunday |

## Notes

# April

| Monday | Tuesday | Wednesday | Thursday | Friday | Saturday | Sunday |
|--------|---------|-----------|----------|--------|----------|--------|
|        |         |           |          | 1      | 2        | 3      |
| 4      | 5       | 6         | 7        | 8      | 9        | 10     |
| 11     | 12      | 13        | 14       | 15     | 16       | 17     |
| 18     | 19      | 20        | 21       | 22     | 23       | 24     |
| 25     | 26      | 27        | 28       | 29     | 30       |        |

Notes

# The Magical Party

Every year when the weather turned warmer, Cinderella put on a special little summer party for all her mice friends.

The mice enjoyed the parties immensely and were so grateful for Cinderella's kindness that they decide to organise a surprise party for her.

So they waited until Cinderella went out on royal business and then rushed to get everything ready.

Quickly, Gus and Jaq wrote out the invitations and sent them to all of Cinderella's friends. 'Come to Cinderella's Magical Party today' read the invitations.

But when it came to organising the rest of the party, the mice found it more difficult. The decorations kept falling down and Lucifer kept chasing the mice out of the kitchen.

It looked as though the party would be a complete disaster and the mice felt very sad.

When Cinderella returned, she

was surprised to see all her friends waiting for her at the palace door.

"We've come for your magical party," declared her stepsister, Drizella.

Cinderella wasn't sure what Drizella was talking about but invited everyone in anyway and stalled them until she could find out what was going on.

She soon found Jaq and Gus hiding in the garden and asked them what was happening.

"We only wanted to do something special and memorable for you," they cried.

"I think it was a very sweet thought," said Cinderella, "but it

will be memorable for all the wrong reasons when I tell those guests there isn't going to be a magical party today."

Just then, they heard a familiar voice on the other side of the bush. "If it is magic you wanted, mice," said the Fairy Godmother, "why didn't you come to me in the first place?"

"You're Cinderella's Fairy Godmother, not ours," squeaked Jaq. "We didn't know we could ask you for help as well."

"I may not be your Fairy Godmother but I am your friend," the Fairy Godmother replied.

Cinderella's friends were just beginning to get restless, when Cinderella returned with the mice and the Fairy Godmother.

"I'd like to thank everyone for coming to my magical party," Cinderella announced.

The crowd gasped, as the Fairy Godmother waved her wand and created an instant party, with a giant cake.

The party was a great success and everyone was happy.

Cinderella thanked the mice for arranging the party and the Fairy Godmother for saving the day.

"We couldn't have made this party any more memorable if we tried," cheered Jaq, as he and Gus congratulated themselves, by tucking into a giant slice of the cake.

## The End

# Cinderella

## Cinderella and Prince Charming

Although Cinderella is gentle and softly spoken, she has a keen intelligence and a sense of humour which she wisely keeps hidden from her jealous stepsisters. Her goodness and beauty are rewarded when her dreams come true and she marries Prince Charming.

## Fairy Godmother

Cinderella's Fairy Godmother is as kind as she is distracted. With her magic words, she makes Cinderella's dreams come true.

## Stepsisters

Dark-haired Drizella and red-headed Anastasia are Cinderella's stepsisters. These two are mean, clumsy and rude. They manage to get along together only when they team up against Cinderella.

## Gus and Jaq

Gus and Jaq care about Cinderella very much. They love to give Cinderella surprises for the simple pleasure of making her happy.

# Tiara Invites

*You'll have a ball creating these princess party invites.*

## You will need:

glitter glue

glue

gold card & wrapping paper

pencil

scissors

**1**

Draw a tiara shape on gold card and carefully cut it out.

Draw a smaller tiara shape on wrapping paper and glue it onto the gold tiara shape.

**Note to parents:** adult supervision is recommended when sharp-pointed items such as scissors are in use.

**2**

**3**

Decorate the front of your invites with glitter glue. Don't forget to write down all the information about your party.

PRINCESS PARTY
Dress code:

PRINCESS PARTY
Dress code: Don't forget your tiara!

# Summer Changes

There are six changes to the picture on the right. Can you spot them?

29

# May

| Monday | Tuesday | Wednesday | Thursday | Friday | Saturday | Sunday |
|--------|---------|-----------|----------|--------|----------|--------|
|        |         |           |          |        |          | 1      |
| 2      | 3       | 4         | 5        | 6      | 7        | 8      |
| 9      | 10      | 11        | 12       | 13     | 14       | 15     |
| 16     | 17      | 18        | 19       | 20     | 21       | 22     |
| 23     | 24      | 25        | 26       | 27     | 28       | 29     |
| 30     | 31      |           |          |        |          |        |

Notes

# June

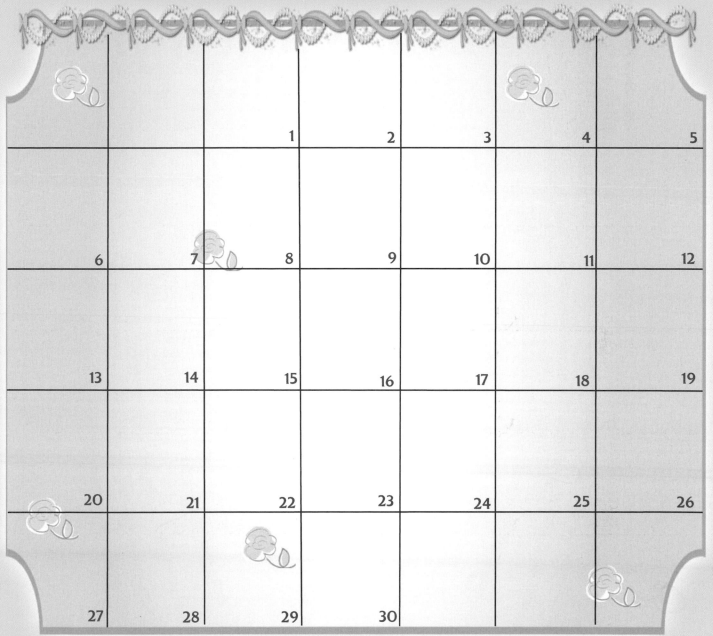

| Monday | Tuesday | Wednesday | Thursday | Friday | Saturday | Sunday |
|--------|---------|-----------|----------|--------|----------|--------|
|  |  | 1 | 2 | 3 | 4 | 5 |
| 6 | 7 | 8 | 9 | 10 | 11 | 12 |
| 13 | 14 | 15 | 16 | 17 | 18 | 19 |
| 20 | 21 | 22 | 23 | 24 | 25 | 26 |
| 27 | 28 | 29 | 30 |  |  |  |

Notes

31

# The Endless Night

It was the height of summer and the Underwater Kingdom was full of life. Everyone was wearing bright colours and enjoying the dazzling lightshows that the sun's rays made through the water.

Ursula knew how much summer meant to the mermaids and came up with an evil plan – to hold it to ransom!

"If I were to steal the sun's light," she cackled, "the Underwater Kingdom would be plunged into an endless night."

So, Ursula used her strongest magical powers to harness the sun's rays and trap them inside her crystal ball.

As soon as Ursula had done this, Ariel and King Triton instantly knew there was something wrong. The sky above the sea's surface had become dark and gloomy. The lack of sunshine made the mermaids and mermen feel downhearted and listless.

Sadly, King Triton realised that the disappearance of the sun represented a much more serious

threat. "Without the sun's warm light, the sea will get colder and colder," he gulped. "Nothing can survive for very long in such conditions."

On cue, Ursula appeared with her crystal ball full of sunshine and made her demands on King Triton.

"Unless you hand over your trident and recognise me as ruler of the seas," hissed Ursula, "you will watch all those you care for perish in the darkness of the endless night."

King Triton had no choice and sadly told Ursula that he would fetch his trident from the palace.

Ariel couldn't bear to watch her father hand over his kingdom and swam away to be alone.

Suddenly, through the gloomy sea, Ariel saw something glowing in the distance. She followed the light down to a cave on the seabed. The light was coming from a friendly, luminous fish. The bright light gave Ariel a glimmer of hope.

Back at the royal palace, King Triton was just about to hand over his trident to Ursula, when Ariel came racing back with the little glowing fish.

"Don't give it to her, Daddy," cried Ariel. "I've found some light!"

King Triton hesitated for a moment and looked at his daughter.

Ursula laughed at Ariel's attempts to thwart her evil plan.

"One little fish can't light up an entire kingdom,"

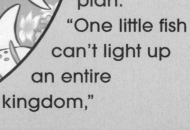

howled Ursula.

"He can with the help of his brothers and sisters," replied Ariel.

With that, a whole shoal of luminous fish arrived and the sea was as bright as day.

Ursula was furious and tried to zap the fish with her powers but King Triton blocked her attack with his trident and Ursula's zap bounced back and gave her a giant shock that left her helpless.

Once Ursula was safely tied up, King Triton took her crystal ball containing the sun's golden light and handed the crystal ball to Ariel.

"Well done, Ariel. You saved us all," said King Triton. "So I think it's only right that you should be the one to return the sunshine."

Ariel swam through the dark sea and up to the surface. When she held the crystal ball up, light exploded in every direction, leaving a glorious sunset and skyline.

"The sunshine somehow seems even brighter and warmer than it did before," commented Ariel.

"That's because the sun is rewarding you for saving the summer, Ariel," laughed King Triton.

## The End

# Ariel

## Ariel and King Triton

With her beauty and bell-like voice, Ariel, King Triton's youngest daughter, should be the perfect princess. In fact, her independent spirit and impulsive nature make her a handful for her father, who tries his best to understand her.

## Flounder and Sebastian

Sebastian is the court composer, not to mention the right-hand man to King Triton, who orders him to keep a watchful eye on Ariel. But Sebastian, who cares for Ariel very much, ends up trying to make her dreams come true. Flounder is Ariel's very best friend. He is loyal and affectionate. Together, they have fun in the sea.

## Ursula

Power-hungry Ursula, the sea-witch, was driven from the palace and ever since then she has longed to make King Triton pay for it ... by taking his place. She has two henchmen called Flotsam and Jetsam.

# Starfish Bangle

*You'll be ready to make a splash when you make and wear this bangle.*

## You will need:

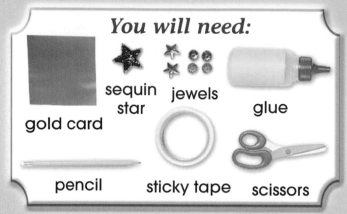

gold card

sequin star

jewels

glue

pencil

sticky tape

scissors

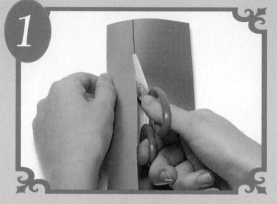

**1**

Draw and cut out a strip of gold card, long enough to go around your wrist.

Decorate the gold strip by gluing on a sequin star and fake jewels.

**Note to parents:** adult supervision is recommended when sharp-pointed items such as scissors are in use.

**2**

**3**

Tape the gold strip into a bangle shape. Now your starfish bangle is ready to wear.

Use the little picture inside the sea-flower to
help you colour this page.

# July

| Monday | Tuesday | Wednesday | Thursday | Friday | Saturday | Sunday |
|--------|---------|-----------|----------|--------|----------|--------|
|  |  |  |  | 1 | 2 | 3 |
| 4 | 5 | 6 | 7 | 8 | 9 | 10 |
| 11 | 12 | 13 | 14 | 15 | 16 | 17 |
| 18 | 19 | 20 | 21 | 22 | 23 | 24 |
| 25 | 26 | 27 | 28 | 29 | 30 | 31 |

Notes

# August

| Monday | Tuesday | Wednesday | Thursday | Friday | Saturday | Sunday |
|--------|---------|-----------|----------|--------|----------|--------|
| 1 | 2 | 3 | 4 | 5 | 6 | 7 |
| 8 | 9 | 10 | 11 | 12 | 13 | 14 |
| 15 | 16 | 17 | 18 | 19 | 20 | 21 |
| 22 | 23 | 24 | 25 | 26 | 27 | 28 |
| 29 | 30 | 31 | | | | |

Notes

# Jasmine's Inspiration

All summer, Jasmine's clothes designs had been the toast of Agrabah.

Her friends marvelled at her inspired use of colour and competed with one another to wear her outfits. The outfits were bright and summery with lots of dazzling jewels.

Even though the clothes had been a big hit all summer, her friends were very eager to see what Jasmine would come up with next.

"We've had these outfits for almost two months, Jasmine," a girl raved. "Every girl in the city is wearing them. We can't wait to see your new collection."

Aladdin knew the secret to Jasmine's inspiration, because he had been helping her. Every weekend he took her far away from the palace on his Magic Carpet. The couple spent romantic dates at a lush oasis which had been full of bright summer flowers and

dazzling creatures.

Jasmine had been observing how the wild colours stood out in the sunshine. "It's just a matter of capturing the feel of the oasis and putting them into my designs," she giggled.

But this time, when they visited the oasis, Jasmine noticed that there were changes everywhere. The bright green leaves had lost their colour. They had turned brown, orange and red. Jasmine picked up a handful of leaves and sighed. She also noticed the fur on the creatures was much

darker and thicker.

"What is happening?" panicked Jasmine. "Is the oasis dying?"

"No, it's just the end of summer and autumn is on its way," explained Aladdin.

"Oh, no, everyone is expecting me to come back with a new range of clothes but all the colours are draining away," she fretted.

After a while, they returned to the palace with the leaves. Jasmine couldn't think of any new designs with the colours she had. And all her friends were pressurising her into showing her new collection.

Jasmine thought that she would never get any inspiration and sadly went out on the balcony to be alone. As she stared out over the land, she saw that the summer light was changing. Everything was more relaxed and subtle. She looked at the colours of the autumn leaves in her hand and had an idea.

"That's it!" she cheered. "I'm trying to think of summer clothes when I should be thinking about an autumn collection." She asked Aladdin to take her back to the oasis. It was full of gold and warm colours. Jasmine was soon inspired and within a few days she was presenting the autumn collection to her friends. They loved the new range of colours. Yet again, Jasmine had stayed one step ahead of the game.

She was so grateful for Aladdin's help that she gave him a heart-shaped ruby with their initials engraved in it. "This is to remind you how I feel about you all year round," Jasmine whispered.

## The End

42

# Jasmine

## Jasmine and Aladdin

Jasmine is an exotic, fiery beauty. She doesn't ask for much – just to marry for love and to experience life outside the palace. Aladdin will need courage and intelligence as great as hers to win and keep this princess's heart.

## Abu and Rajah

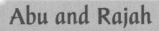

Abu is Aladdin's friendly and inventive pet monkey. At first, he is jealous of Jasmine but then she wins his heart. Rajah is Jasmine's big kitten. He is her only true friend at the palace.

## The Sultan

The Sultan is Jasmine's father. He is friendly, funny, naive and adores his daughter so much that he changes the law to allow Jasmine to be with Aladdin.

# Mirror of Jewels

*Create this mirror of jewels – it's perfect for your room at the palace.*

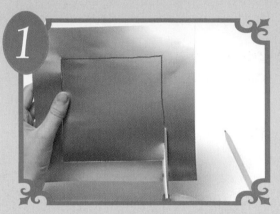

**1** Cut a square from gold card, then draw and cut out a smaller square in the centre.

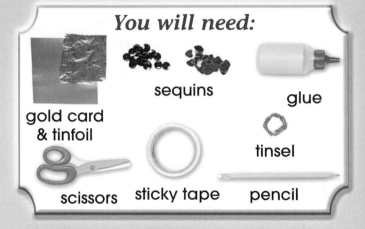

## You will need:

gold card & tinfoil

sequins

glue

tinsel

scissors

sticky tape

pencil

**Note to parents:** adult supervision is recommended when sharp-pointed items such as scissors are in use.

Cut a large square of tinfoil and glue it to the back of the gold square.

**2**

**3**

Decorate the front of the gold square with sequins and tinsel. Hang your mirror in pride of place in your room.

# Autumn Wishes

*Solve these teasers and discover what Jasmine has wished for.*

**1** Which piece of cord leads to which item?

**2** Unscramble the letters to discover Jasmine's autumn wish.

H S A W L A

**3** Can you complete these sums?

a   20   +   15   = $\boxed{85}$

b   7   x   7   = $\boxed{12}$

c   29   -   6   = $\boxed{1}$

d   4   x   3   = $\boxed{\phantom{0}}$

**4** Write down all the light blue letters to reveal a secret word.

| S | C | D | K | L | U | S | F |
|---|---|---|---|---|---|---|---|
| D | K | E | S | W | F | J | A |
| V | E | G | V | K | O | P | S |
| G | E | I | W | Q | W | X | C |
| Z | B | M | N | A | Y | S | R |

Answers:
1) Cord 'a' leads to the ring, cord 'b' leads to the necklace, cord 'c' leads to the bangle. 2) Jasmine's autumn wish is for a shawl. 3) a-35, b-49, c-23, d-12. 4) The secret word is LEAVES.

# September

| Monday | Tuesday | Wednesday | Thursday | Friday | Saturday | Sunday |
|---|---|---|---|---|---|---|
| | | | 1 | 2 | 3 | 4 |
| 5 | 6 | 7 | 8 | 9 | 10 | 11 |
| 12 | 13 | 14 | 15 | 16 | 17 | 18 |
| 19 | 20 | 21 | 22 | 23 | 24 | 25 |
| 26 | 27 | 28 | 29 | 30 | | |

Notes

# October

| Monday | Tuesday | Wednesday | Thursday | Friday | Saturday | Sunday |
|--------|---------|-----------|----------|--------|----------|--------|
| | | | | 1 | 2 | |
| 3 | 4 | 5 | 6 | 7 | 8 | 9 |
| 10 | 11 | 12 | 13 | 14 | 15 | 16 |
| 17 | 18 | 19 | 20 | 21 | 22 | 23 |
| 24 | 25 | 26 | 27 | 28 | 29 | 30 |
| 31 | | | | | | |

## Notes

# The Snowy Day

One morning, Belle looked out of the window and saw that it had snowed during the night. She couldn't wait to go outside and have fun.

Belle asked the Beast to come with her but he refused.

"I never go out in the snow and you shouldn't either!" he grumbled.

"Why not?" replied Belle.

"Because it's far too cold and dangerous," shuddered the Beast. "Everything is freezing, slippery and you might catch a bad cold!"

Belle protested but the Beast got angry and forbade her to leave the castle.

Of course, this made Belle even more determined to go outside in the snow.

"You might be scared of having some fun … but I'm not," she declared, as she left the

castle with Chip.

"Fine!" the Beast fumed. "When you get in trouble, don't expect me to help you."

At first Belle and Chip were having a great time in the snow. The branches on the trees were full of dangling icicles. Belle thought that the icicles looked just like diamond jewellery draped on the trees. "They look like princess trees," she giggled to Chip.

All of a sudden, they both sank into a deep snowdrift and couldn't get out.

"Oh dear, I should have listened to the Beast's warning," Belle gulped, as they slowly sank deeper.

Meanwhile, back at the castle, the Beast was still sulking because Belle had defied him. But suddenly, the hair on the back of his neck tingled; he sensed that Belle was in danger. He grabbed the magic mirror and ordered, "Show me Belle!" The Beast gasped when he saw in the mirror what had happened to Belle. The Beast put his anger and fear aside and raced to help Belle. He soon pulled her and Chip out of the snowdrift.

"You were right," shivered Belle. "We shouldn't have come out in the snow."

"No, I was wrong, Belle," replied the Beast. "I should have put aside my dislike for the cold weather and come along to keep you safe."

"Well, now that you are here maybe I can help change your mind about the snow?" suggested Belle.

So Belle and the Beast had a snowball fight, then a ride on a sledge and visited a secret ice cave.

As they walked back to the castle, Belle and the Beast held hands.

"Thanks, Belle. I've had a great time in the snow but I don't understand why I'm not feeling cold at all," puzzled the Beast.

"Because you're happy and have a warm heart," replied Belle.

"My heart feels warm because I'm near you," admitted the Beast.

"Well, why do you think I asked you to come in the first place?" giggled Belle. "That's how you make my heart feel, too."

## The End

# Belle

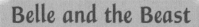

## Belle and the Beast

Belle is as lovely as her name implies but her natural beauty is more than skin deep. When the Beast finally wins her trust, she gives him all the kindness and patience he deserves.

## Mrs Potts and Chip

Mrs Potts is the castle cook who was turned into a comical teapot. She is romantic, cheerful and optimistic. She is not afraid of the Beast because she sees his pain and she helps both Belle and the Beast understand each other. Chip is a cup and is Mrs Potts' son; he is the perfect example of childhood innocence.

## Lumiere and Cogsworth

Lumiere is a charming French candelabra with a burning desire to make his guests feel at home. Cogsworth is a mantle clock who performs his duties as head servant in a timely and orderly manner.

# Sparkling Star

*Create this Christmas decoration –
it sparkles just like a real star.*

**1**

Ask an adult to break the pegs in half. Spread glue over the pegs and cover with glitter. Leave to dry.

## You will need:

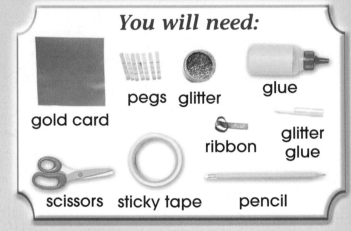

gold card · pegs · glitter · glue · ribbon · glitter glue · scissors · sticky tape · pencil

**Princess Tip**
Lay a sheet of paper down before you begin.

**Note to parents:** adult supervision is recommended when sharp-pointed items such as scissors are in use.

Arrange the pegs in a star and glue onto a circle of gold card. Decorate another gold circle with glitter glue and glue on top.

**2**

**3**

Glue the gold circle to the centre of the star. Cut a length of ribbon and make it into a loop, then tape to the back of the star.

Use the little picture inside the Christmas
wreath to help you colour this page.

# November

|  |  |  |  |  |  |  |
|---|---|---|---|---|---|---|
| 1 | 2 | 3 | 4 | 5 | 6 | |
| 7 | 8 | 9 | 10 | 11 | 12 | 13 |
| 14 | 15 | 16 | 17 | 18 | 19 | 20 |
| 21 | 22 | 23 | 24 | 25 | 26 | 27 |
| 28 | 29 | 30 | | | | |

Monday  Tuesday  Wednesday  Thursday  Friday  Saturday  Sunday

Notes

# December

| Monday | Tuesday | Wednesday | Thursday | Friday | Saturday | Sunday |
|---|---|---|---|---|---|---|
| | | | Ingrid's Birthday 1 | 2 | 3 | 4 |
| 5 | 6 | 7 | 8 | 9 | 10 | 11 |
| 12 | 13 | 14 | 15 | 16 | 17 | 18 |
| 19 | 20 | 21 | 22 | 23 | Christmas Eve 24 | Christmas Day 25 |
| Boxing Day 26 | Hannah Birthday 27 | Louise birthday 28 | 29 | 30 | 31 | |

## Notes

# The New Year Search

*Fill your name in the blank spaces in the story below.*

It was almost New Year and Mulan went to the Emperor's palace to join the celebrations. Young girls from all over China had come for the big occasion. Mulan noticed a very pretty girl called _____. The Emperor called all the girls together and made an

announcement. He showed them a beautiful flower. "This is a brand new type of flower especially grown for the coming New Year," the Emperor said. "At present it has no name. It will be named after the girl who can show me the most important thing that anyone can discover at the start of any New

Year."

The girls rushed off to search for ideas.

Mulan picked a bunch of ancient flowers. "Putting the older flowers with the new will show that the past is not forgotten," thought Mulan, "the same way that each new generation should honour their Ancestors."

Unfortunately, Mulan bumped into _____ who had the same idea.

When the other girls saw Mulan and _____ with flowers, they started picking them, too.

"Now no one will win with that idea," sighed _____ .

So they decided to separate and go in search of another idea.

Mulan decided that a ribbon dance would be a great way of showing that time was always moving.

"I'll do lots of spectacular moves with the

ribbon before the dance ends," declared Mulan. "Then I shall explain that we can do just as many exciting things before this New Year ends."

"Oh, dear. I was going to do exactly the same thing," gasped _____ . She had been practising with a ribbon, too!

"If we keep having the same ideas," sighed Mulan, "neither of us will win."

So _____ suggested that they kept out of each other's way until the performance. "If we're in different places we'll both think of different things," said _____ .

So Mulan went and sat by a blossom tree. The falling petals continually floated down around her. This gave Mulan another idea.

"I'm sure

_____ won't think of doing another dance, so I will," said Mulan. "Each falling petal is completely individual and beautiful. This will remind us that each day of the coming year should be just as individual."

It was soon time for the performances in front of the Emperor.

"Who has made the best New Year's discovery and will have the flower named after them?" mused the Emperor.

Mulan had put on a petal print dress and was waiting to go on stage but she was stunned when _____ appeared wearing a very similar outfit.

"You're not going to do a petal dance, too, are you?"

gasped Mulan.

"Yes, this is terrible, because we're so alike we keep spoiling each other's plans!"_____ sighed.

"There's only one thing for it," laughed Mulan. "We should just enjoy ourselves and work as a team."

The girls thought they had no chance of winning together but they had become friends and had a great time performing their identical dances in front of the Emperor.

To their surprise and delight, the Emperor applauded their dance and presented them with the flower. "The most important thing that anyone can discover at the start of a New Year is a new friend," smiled the Emperor, and named the flower after Mulan and _____.

**The End**

# Mulan

## Mulan and Shang

Although Mulan is as lovely as a blossom flower, she can't seem to behave like the demure daughter she is supposed to be. In fact, she is quite the tomboy. Shang, a captain in the Imperial army, likes Mulan and a firm friendship grows.

## Cri-Kee and Mushu

Cri-Kee is a cricket and he is Mulan's companion through thick and thin. Mushu is a tiny, self-important dragon who can talk his way through anything.

## Khan and Little Brother

Khan is Mulan's horse. He is like a watchful parent and never strays too far from her side. Little Brother is Mulan's pet dog. He is adorable but not so bright. He generally loves Mulan and is the only one who doesn't question Mulan's ways – even if she does use him to do her chores.

# Fabulous Fan

*You'll look like a Chinese princess when you make and hold this fan.*

### You will need:

stapler     scissors

wrapping paper     pencil

**1**

Draw and cut out a square from pretty wrapping paper.

**Note to parents:** adult supervision is recommended when sharp-pointed items such as scissors are in use.

**2**

Make a fold in the paper, then turn the paper over and make another fold. Repeat this until all the paper is folded.

**3**

Staple the fan into shape with a stapler. Hold the fan like an oriental princess.

# New Year Princess

*Help Mulan solve these New Year puzzles.*

**1**

Who is Little Brother?

a) Mulan's little brother
b) Mulan's pet dog
c) Mulan's friend

**2**

When is New Year's Day?

a) 31st December
b) 30th December
c) 1st January

In the space below, draw what you think Mulan's New Year wish might be.

**3**

Where does Mulan like to sit in her family garden?

a) On a bench
b) Under the blossom tree
c) On her swing

**4**

What is Mulan's family name?

a) Fa
b) Pa
c) La

2007 **2004** 2003

2006

- **My favourite moment this year** I am moveing house and I have got a boy frend and I am going to Love him!

- **My favourite party this year**

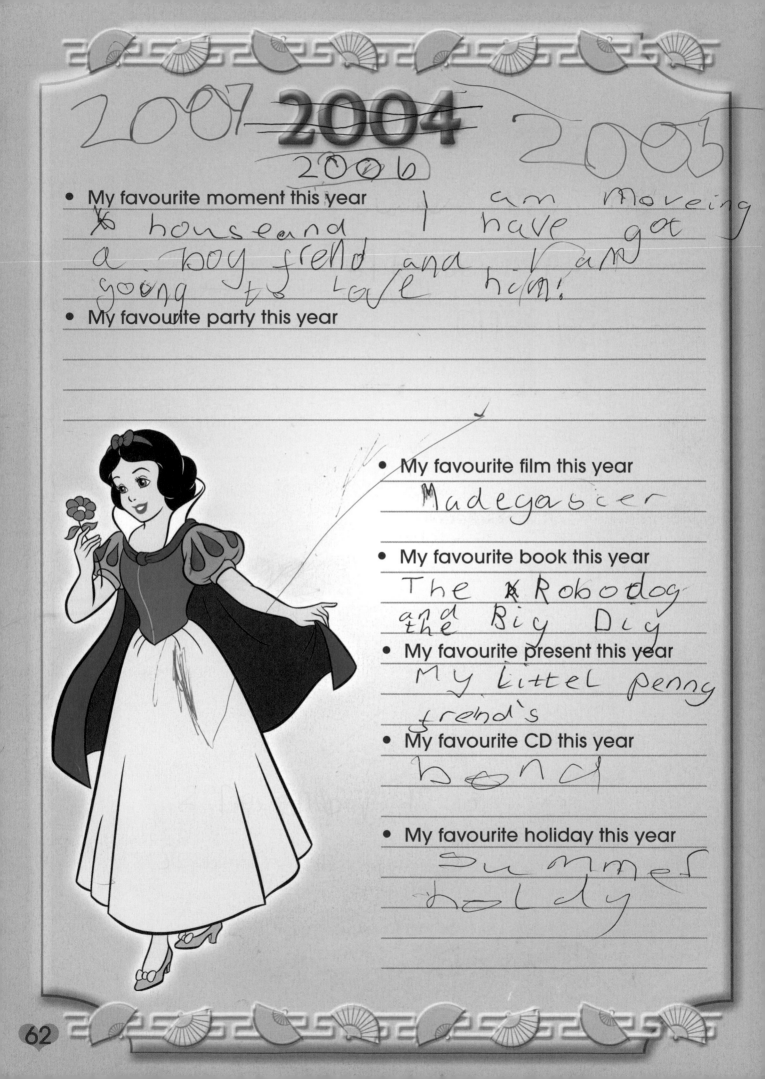

- **My favourite film this year**
  Madegasier

- **My favourite book this year**
  The Robo dog and Big Dig

- **My favourite present this year**
  My littel penny frend's

- **My favourite CD this year**
  band

- **My favourite holiday this year**
  Summer holdy

# 2005

2007

2007

2007

200

- My New Year's resolution

_____

_____

_____

_____

_____

_____

- My wishes, hopes and dreams

_____

_____

_____

_____

_____

_____

_____

_____

_____

_____

_____

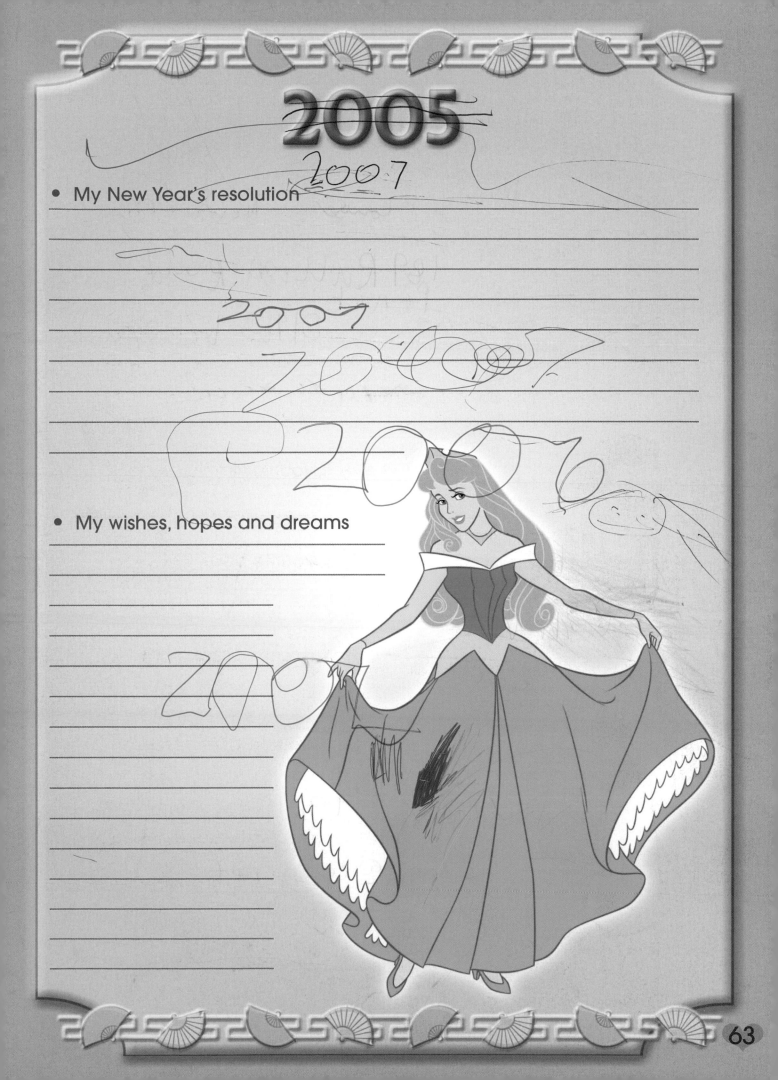

# All About Me

- Her Royal Highness, Princess  Louise    Newberry

- Address of royal palace  189 Rullion Road Penick

- Telephone  01968 676 046

- Mobile

- Eye colour  brown

- Hair colour  brown

- Height

- Star sign

- Birthday  28 December 1998

- E-mail  stephen.newberry@tesco.net

- Signature  Louise

**A photograph or drawing of me**

# My Best Friend

- Her Royal Highness, Princess

- Address of royal palace

- Telephone

- Mobile

**A photograph or drawing of my friend**

- E-mail

- Her favourite colour is

- Her favourite animal is

- Her favourite band is

- Her favourite film is

- Her favourite book is

- Her favourite sport is

# Beautiful Birthdays

- Princess/Prince Hannah D.

- Birthday December 27,

- Star sign

- Ideal presents

- Princess/Prince

- Birthday

- Star sign

- Ideal presents

- Princess/Prince

- Birthday

- Star sign

- Ideal presents

- Princess/Prince melanie N.

- Birthday Oct 1

- Star sign

- Ideal presents

- Princess/Prince

- Birthday

- Star sign

- Ideal presents

- Princess/Prince

- Birthday

- Star sign

- Ideal presents

# Princess School

- My school  Torban Primery Schod
- Address  Whillyim sealers Street 13
- Telephone  01968 675045
- My year  December
- My class  4 or 5

- Headteacher
- Favourite subject  Maths
- Worst subject
- Favourite teacher
- Least favourite teacher
- Best school lunch
- Worst school lunch

# Princess Quiz

Have you ever wondered which princess you are most like?
Play this game to find out. All you need is a counter.

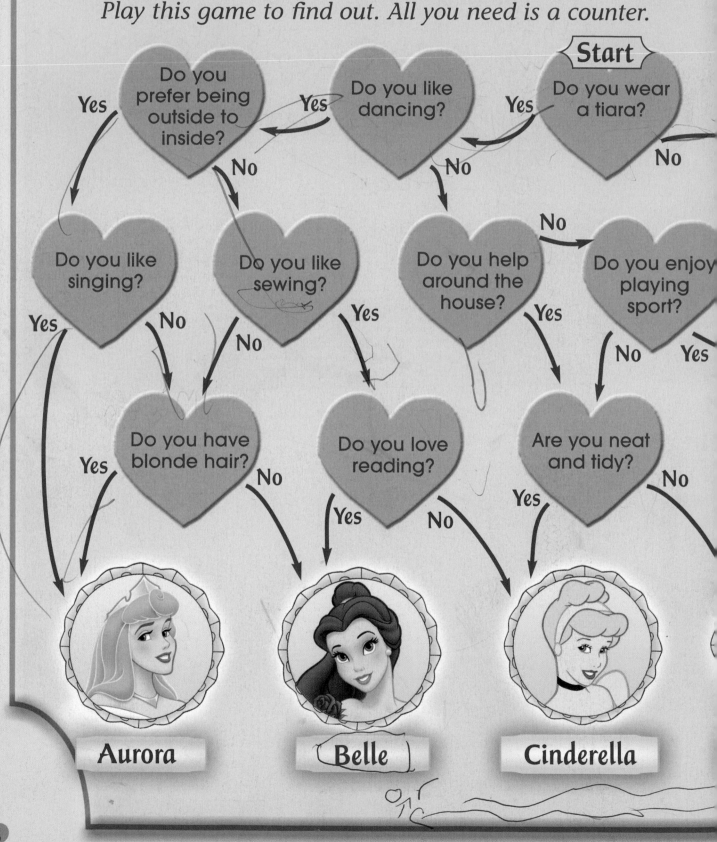

**Start**
Do you wear a tiara?

Do you like dancing?

Do you prefer being outside to inside?

Do you like singing?

Do you like sewing?

Do you help around the house?

Do you enjoy playing sport?

Do you have blonde hair?

Do you love reading?

Are you neat and tidy?

Yes — Yes — Yes — No — No — No — No — Yes — No — Yes — No — Yes — Yes — Yes — No — Yes — No — Yes — No — Yes — No

**Aurora**

**Belle**

**Cinderella**

# How to play

Place your counter at the start. Answer the question, then follow the correct arrow to move your counter to the next question. Continue until you reach a princess. You are most like this princess.

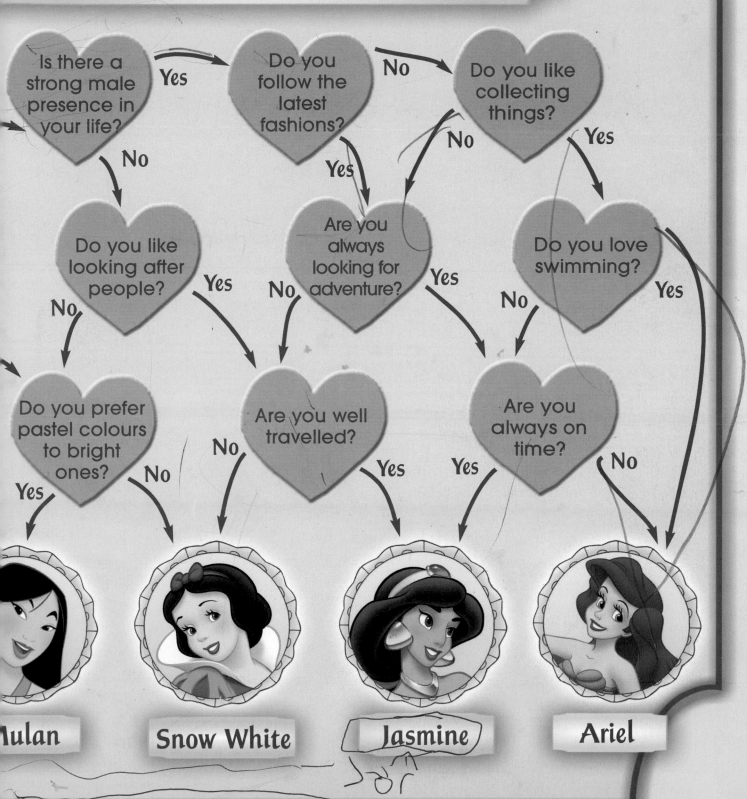

Is there a strong male presence in your life? — Yes → Do you follow the latest fashions?

Is there a strong male presence in your life? — No ↓ Do you like looking after people?

Do you follow the latest fashions? — No → Do you like collecting things?

Do you follow the latest fashions? — Yes ↓ Are you always looking for adventure?

Do you like collecting things? — No → Are you always looking for adventure?

Do you like collecting things? — Yes → Do you love swimming?

Do you like looking after people? — No ↓ Do you prefer pastel colours to bright ones?

Do you like looking after people? — Yes → Are you well travelled?

Are you always looking for adventure? — No ↓ Are you well travelled?

Are you always looking for adventure? — Yes → Are you always on time?

Do you love swimming? — No ↓ Are you always on time?

Do you love swimming? — Yes → Ariel

Do you prefer pastel colours to bright ones? — Yes ↓ Mulan

Do you prefer pastel colours to bright ones? — No → Snow White

Are you well travelled? — No ↓ Snow White

Are you well travelled? — Yes → Jasmine

Are you always on time? — Yes → Jasmine

Are you always on time? — No → Ariel

**Mulan**   **Snow White**   **Jasmine**   **Ariel**

69